Voices from the First Gilded Age

poems by

Ed Granger

Finishing Line Press
Georgetown, Kentucky

Voices from the First Gilded Age

Copyright © 2019 by Ed Granger
ISBN 978-1-64662-062-3 First Edition
All rights reserved under International and Pan-American Copyright Conventions. No part of this book may be reproduced in any manner whatsoever without written permission from the publisher, except in the case of brief quotations embodied in critical articles and reviews.

ACKNOWLEDGMENTS

I am especially grateful to Sue Ellen Thompson, Jenn Givhan, Elise Hempel, Le Hinton, Barrett Warner, and Meg Eden for their support and mentorship. And to my mom.

Publisher: Leah Maines
Editor: Christen Kincaid
Cover Art: Molly Wright, mollywrightart.com
Author Photo: Maddie Granger
Cover Design: Elizabeth Maines McCleavy

Printed in the USA on acid-free paper.
Order online: www.finishinglinepress.com
   also available on amazon.com

Author inquiries and mail orders:
Finishing Line Press
P. O. Box 1626
Georgetown, Kentucky 40324
U. S. A.

Table of Contents

Postmark: London, July 12, 1890 1

Postmark: Paris, August 9, 1892 2

Paris Postcard: Rue Baltard, 1892 3

Postmark: London, July 8, 1893 4

Postmark: Paris, September 15, 1894 5

Paris Postcard: Avenue du Bois de Boulogne, 1896 6

Postmark: Vernon, France., October 1, 1897 7

Postmark: New York, August 12, 1899 8

Paris Postcard: Exposition Universelle, 1900 9

Postmark: Nottingham, November 25, 1901 10

Postmark: London, June 30, 1904 11

Paris Postcard: Pont au Change et le Palais de Justice, 1905 12

Postmark: London, May 8, 1908 13

Postmark: London, April 7, 1909 14

Postmark: Café-Restaurant de la Régence, 1910 15

Postmark: Nottingham, August 2, 1910 16

Postmark: London, January 5, 1911 17

Paris Postcard: Ruelle Sourdis et Rue de Beauce, 1911 18

Postmark: New York, April 19, 1912 19

Postcard, Cornish Riveria Series:
    Portsgatho, Nr. Falmouth, Cornwall, 1912 20

Postmark: Paris, August 2, 1914 21

Postmark: Compiègne, June 23, 1918 22

Postmark: Paris, September 6, 1918 23

Postmark, New York, September 12, 1919 24

Historical Notes 25

for Maddie

*She had everything she wanted, but she still felt, at times,
that there were other things she might want
if she knew about them.*

—Edith Wharton, "The Custom of the Country"

Postmark: London, July 12, 1890

Dear Mabel,
In my next letter, I hope to tell you how I've conquered London, but first, a few lines about our splendid voyage over. Father so talked up "City of New York" that I was sure she'd never measure up to dear Manhattan. Even he looked like the wind had left his sails when our carriage reached the docks and he saw her dowdy bowsprit—"damned old fashioned" were his exact words. But oh, Mabel, the wonders she unfolded when we left the footman wrestling with our trunks and went aboard —I could not have been more astounded if 5th Avenue itself had magically appeared within! Our "cabin" was a suite made up as velvet parlor by day with divans folding neatly into beds. The main saloon was a marvel, with a great arched stained glass roof enclosed at night in iron to show off its electric lights. Or so father reported—we'd been in the ladies drawing room, with its ingenious portholes that cleverly reverse: stained glass by day, then evening mirrors to reflect the glory of the assembled dresses—the better to size up my competition, mother said. Which reminds me, I saw Miss V looking superbly rosy and practicing her French. That girl will take some beating, but mother says I've got the "go" and "snap" the English boys are looking for, poor bored things. According to father, "City of New York" carries 1,740 passengers, but that can't be right, I never saw more than several hundred. But then, I never saw the cooks or butchers, either, or the men down below shoveling father's coal into those marvelous new twin-screwed engines.
Yours,
Alice

Postmark: Paris, August 9, 1892

Dear Sis,
I have to tell you of my recent evening
at Mrs. L's salon, you know the one
the papers cry out as a den of anarchists
and operatic rake-charmers. It's all of it
true, down to the vaunted portrait artist who
it's said knows all his subjects from the inside
out, so to speak (but of course don't speak
of this to mother, or to cousin Jen, who'd
be here in a White Star flash). I even met
that painter whose every landscape is a sad
gray muddle with a splash of crimson
reflected like a death wound in the Thames.
Quite a fascinating fellow, actually, even
less in love with Old New England than I am.
He now does sittings on commission that make
even Lady Meux seem quite demure. We stood
together while a soprano wearing just a bit
more than her own vibrato delivered excerpts
from a new Italian score, discussing our mothers.
In any case, believe what you read in the papers.
Sincerely,
Fred

Paris Postcard: Rue Baltard, 1892

Les Halles unfurls from left edge
to center distance a la Renaissance
perspective, articulate block-long facade
of steel and glass rhythmic as train-click,
arch-to-arch-to-arch transmitting energy
of market day transmuting the feeble
sky blue—tinted by hand: *pochoir*—to green
infusing trees spaced like sentries to affirm
the building's vertices their trunks sprung
from a row of carts backed up to unload
while dwarfed horses wait in traces
for replacement by more steel and glass
and the ancient church of Saint-Eustache
peers over the coop-like roof, lifts
a monocle eye to await its tithe. But
no one in this teeming street looks up.

Postmark: London, July 8, 1893

My Dear Walter,
I trust this letter finds your smelting
going well, and the Aristolochia on which
I've staked my March return continuing
to climb. Speaking of which, I've excellent
news to report: a Duke's become besotted
with our Margaret, and not one of your
recent peerage types. I've seen his country
estate in Shropshire, and despite a touch
of mold and dampness in his stairwell it's
lined with family oils that check out well
according to your man in London as to
size and artist's reputation. I believe this
finally could be her match. She's a mite
reluctant, poor callow girl, as is to be
expected considering her Gentleman
exceeds her years by two decades and a bit.
I'm sure you'll concur the milliner's bills
have not been excessive, nor those from
the dressmaker in Paris—if you but knew
how we economize! I ask this one
concession to our reputation realizing
she's always been your pet. It's time
we put our family's future first. Please
wire earliest regarding a generous dowry.
I remain your affectionate,
Millicent

Postmark: Paris, September 15, 1894

Dear Sis,
I'm booked on the next boat back
to drab old London, where all facades
are furrowed like our father's brow.
And anyhow, who's he to choose
the fate of spirits free as yours and mine?
I know, the last mite's ring does tend
to bring one round to the grim state
of one's coffers—i.e. Connecticut.
A month in Paris and the sea grows infinite.
My love to all hove to in the Colonies.
Yours,
Fred
P.S. Be a brick and plead my case—
I promise I'll find you a Count.

Paris Postcard: Avenue du Bois de Boulogne, 1896

Wide vista issues toward us from the distance
camera's eye placed perfectly so the whole
gay promenade swells to foreground precisely
from the gray mouth of Arc de Triomphe trees
billowing like green smoke from a locomotive so
shade and shadow cool one side of the broad sand-
colored path along which a Sunday throng ebbs
and flows all in hats with parasols shaped like spider's
webs women hidden by dresses that gently cone to cover
even feet except for one toe of the next step men
walking tucked-in trim with canes and boat hats as
almost every face tilts down against sun or breeze or
approaching century that might replace even these
carriages that line the street emerging from left
edge back from the races at Longchamp rolling
to thread l'Arc its central void poised like a needle's
oval eye to wink them laughing back into the past.

Postmark: Vernon, France, October 1, 1897

Dear Papa,
Summer never really ends over here in
Giverny, just grows muddled about its edges,
like grandpapa after he'd kept his
coachman dozing half the night outside
one of his clubs. I'm not sure whether
that makes me grandmamma or the poor
coachman in this case, but the sheer routine
of life here has its compensations. For instance,
the stables know to have my mare saddled
and bridled precisely at seven, before the men
are down to breakfast. By noon, the shadows
in the sitting room recede so it's ideal for reading.
All the servants learn just what one wants,
and when, and if not, there's nothing quite so
instructive as scorn blazing from the green eyes
of a matriarch whose soul has long been given
over to the running of this house. Even the tiny
mouse who cowers behind the tapestries until
she's well in bed knows his place. I realize
that doesn't answer the question of your last
letter as to my happiness. I think I am. Edouard
is very kind. The land for miles around yields
willingly its moods, if not its seasons. The library
is a dream for a girl brought up on Whitman,
Alcott, Thoreau—although I must confess an
odd midnight desire to steal a bit of cheese.
Yours,
Lillian

Postmark: New York, August 12, 1899

Dear Sis,
Imagine my astonishment upon landing
back in fair New York to discover, barely
off the dock, a photograph of Miss Jennie C
in a shop window next to Lillie Langtry's
well-circulated charms. No bare arms yet
rather vulgar, n'cest pas? I've been getting
blown about for two damned years in Pont-Aven,
drawing on father's line at Barclays, straining
to grasp the slippery light as the boats come in.
Admittedly, I'm working with the least compliant
box of paints that Sennelier's yet sold and a teacher
who greets every question by cupping hand to ear
as though I'm pointless as the surf. I'll never pin
those gorgeous Breton forms to paper even
with a unicorn-tipped brush. I realize that now.
But what to make of Jennie, who we once played
whist with back in Cleveland? She's a very lovely
girl, it's true, and she's got Manhattan tucked
beneath her gold-haired spell. Still, it's tough
for me to swallow how shop window space can
go to someone merely known for being famous.
Sincerely,
Fred

Paris Postcard: Exposition Universelle, 1900

Aerial view of Trocadéro taken from atop
the Eiffel Tower, as if a massive table
has been laid by France's most eclectic
pastry chef—architectural array of layer cakes,
baked Alaskas, tiramisus, strudels, petite fours,
profiterole, baklava, zefir-like domes, spun
sugar panes, cannoli columns, spires magicked
from the most exquisitely whipped meringues.
And as pièce de résistance, at center horizon
the Trocadéro Palace lifts her towers in mock
surrender to 50 million tourists as her lower tier
of honeycomb drones with elites who'll stumble
home to keep Europe blissful in its hyperglycemia.

Postmark: Nottingham, November 25, 1901

Dear Mother,
First of all, I want to reassure you
Dr. Daniels did his best. Yet there may be
wisdom in this necessity for women
to greet lust and its inevitable aftermath
with demure smiles. One never knows how
it will all turn out, and the whole world
needn't know, either. No announcement
in the papers means no explanation
when there's no blessed event. William has
also reassured me there's no blame, and we'll
soon try again for an heir. For now, there's just
this memory the wracking pain could not blot
out of how I bled for hours and hours and hours.
With Deepest Regret,
Margaret

Postmark: London, June 30, 1904

Dear Henry,
Mother seems quite determined I'll
earn us a coronet this season. I've been
measured, weighed, and ogled at least
twice by every young titled man in England,
and most of the gray wolves as well.
And it would be too soon if I'm never
invited to tea again in some stuffy room
with a view of buildings surely designed by
the same dull minds that invented hat boxes.
I'd give my chance at an earl for a cool green
afternoon on the Hudson with you and the rest
of our old set—people who comprehend
the need for art and laughter. Oh, but I'm sure
you'll find this droll—father fired off three
telegrams in quick succession as though he was
back in command of his frigate sending a shot
across the bow of some Rebel sloop making a run
for Charleston. He'd gotten a bill for two dozen
pair of kid gloves and assumed mother had lost
all sense of an American dollar's sacred worth.
Poor man, he didn't know you can only wear
them once—so paper-thin I can see the outline
of my nails in chandelier light. Skin must
never touch skin. It's as if each waltz is slowly
making me a ghost inside my own reflection.
Your Loving Sister,
Sarah

Paris Postcard: Pont au Change et le Palais de Justice, 1905

Bridge sweeps across the Seine from lower
right to open out the view of le Palais which
is of necessity regular as justice insisting
on earnest consistency with a grid of sharply
delineated windows and floors as if it forms
a stencil that could be laid atop chaos to reveal
order, yet with a twin flourish of turrets
as though a mill's been built to grind the grist
of theft and grift while across the street
a showy columned tribute to excess is topped
with a Fabergé egg. The bridge railing itself
repeats le Palais with its vertical metal figure
bent like a question mark growing smaller
and smaller until it blurs at the far bank once
it's finished asking its question of the row
of straw hats and bonnets repeated all along
the rail like an answer stamped by the retailers
of France as everyone peers below where
a bateau enters or emerges from a thrice-
repeated arch and between each arch
the imperial seal of Napoleon III vouches
for continuity and no one's marching yet just
standing as if justice is itself a kind of
stasis and is actually being done over and over
in this very scene because nothing changes
and no one, no one, no one, tries to jump.

Postmark: London, May 8, 1908

Dear Cousin Maddie,
These rooms grow ever more familiar in this
ceaseless rain, but no more habitable. I hadn't
noticed when I moved in that the basin
has a tiny crack from drain to lip as if some bit
of brokenness once made a run for it then flung
itself to the floor. Indeed, the carpet looks
as if it's welcomed many a headlong
visitor—not quite as threadbare as these
ochre muslin drapes, but well on its way.
Then there are the pensive faces of the lions
whose well-rubbed heads guard both andirons.
My life lately revolves around this fireplace.
I suppose every young man thwarted in his hopes
for love and all that must ensue like a bright
locomotive set firm upon its tracks has found his
surroundings dimming in his estimation. Yet
I am, I admit, still quite taken aback by Helen's
failure to alight last month at Paddington.
Which reminds me, have you heard from Ellen?
I wonder how she took it when I sailed for London.
Sincerely,
Charlie

Postmark: London, April 7, 1909

Dear Henry,
I'm just back from seeing Ann, our cousin
uncle Michael's self-made millions have made
into Lady Wallingford. Oh Hen, the poor girl's
miserable, miles from London that may as well
be centuries, especially considering the way her
new Earl's Oxfordshire estate has been filled
willy-nilly, as if his forebears had pilfered
a series of French generals then topped the lot
with bits from India, Gibraltar, and an Algerian
bazaar. It's absurd how the servants plot
to make her seem incompetent while the library
has but one good fireplace. It's all downright
Neanderthal. Although I did accidentally
discover a little gem of a Corot cowering in
the Butler's pantry. Poor un-gilded thing. Which
reminds me, on my way back into Mauretania's
vulgar arms, I stopped at Duveen's unbeknownst
to father. What I saw there sufficed to feed my soul
for a lifetime: Fra Angelico's by the score, unknown
da Vinci sketches, new works by Matisse, Gauguin,
Utrillo, our American, Cassatt. I'm still reeling.
Do you suppose father would let me replace
his man in London? I've already shown
that incompetent how the brushstrokes on papa's
long-sought Bartolommeo reveal it as a fake.
I'll never consign myself to a latter-day Bastille
like Ann—all those trips to Rome and Florence
we took together for "refinement" only for her
to languish in a grim pastoral Pleistocene. Papa
must regret the thousands spent on my "first-rate"
education, or yet thank me for them. I'm prepared
to pursue this whim, even to my own extinction.
Your Determined Sister,
Sarah

Paris Postcard: Café-Restaurant de la Régence, 1910

Spacious, clean, airy, and neat—no
skirmish of tables clenched between
outside wall and passing feet but a place
of curious calm, careful proportion,
oasis of simple wooden chairs arranged
at rectangular tables as if paired for
an old allemande or courante, the bar
in its carved somber curve, a few hanging
plants, one urned fern. But this scene flatters
to deceive, eye of a storm soon resumed yet
silent when in mere hours disciples
of the great Philidor will sit bent over thirty
boards as pawns scuttle into no man's
land and kings glare across at their
truculent cousins. And where are the next great
commanders of France? Down in Saumur
perfecting the cavalry charge. Check. Mate.

Postmark: Nottingham, August 2, 1910

Dear Father,
William's just been reelected as MP,
which you may well have expected,
but it was, as Wellington once said,
"the nearest run thing." While he
was down in London working to
stave off ill-timed reforms some
upstart dared to stand for his seat.
There was nothing for it but to set
out in William's sister's tandem we'd
decked out in ribbons proclaiming
Willie's Aintree racing colors. It was
exhilarating, father, racing round our
borough, making speeches—something
I'd never be allowed to do back home.
It helped that Willie often talks politics
with me "as if you'd been born a Tory,"
so I explained to him I was raised one.
Your Affectionate,
Margaret

Postmark: London, January 5, 1911

Dear Grandfather,
I can't help but think of your initial dip
into England's steady currency every time
I set foot in the dear old Langham and run
my palms along the wrought iron rails our
family's ironworks wrought for them. It's as if
Pittsburgh's smokestacks smote the infamous
London fog. When everyone advised "go
West," you went against the grain, which is why
the irony of reading in the papers of a shootout
last night in the East End compels me to write.
It was apparently a gang of Latvians, mostly
Jews and anarchists, who believe that robbery
and murder are justified since private property
is not. It's as if Billy the Kid was in the right
of things, or those Hungarians who tried to shut
our plant down once. In this instance, the police
were hopelessly out-gunned until the Home
Secretary arrived to smoke them out. I'm certain
from the photos in the papers it was Winston,
Jennie Jerome's son—did you not once hint
at scandal that forced the family to abandon
Brooklyn? The Times suggests he overstepped
his bounds, but perhaps that runs in one's
blood. The lesson on all sides of this debacle
seems to be: one's pedigree will out.
Sincerely,
George

Paris Postcard: Ruelle Sourdis et Rue de Beauce, 1911

Buildings loom sheer at either edge as we
slip through a crack in the impeccable
smile of the "City of Light" into a dim realm
hidden as the obverse of a 10-franc piece.
"Ouverte en 1626"—this street is no more
than a dozen feet across, leading us on past
a slouching man in uniform (soldat? gendarme?)
wall to our left pierced by two small square dark
apertures, right wall with lower level iron-barred,
several doors almost lost in profile, shutters
above where the walls converge
to squeeze the light into a distant misty
keyhole slot that rises from an arch
into a narrow channel then
a notch, another channel,
another notch,
seeks
a widening, room
to breathe, the key to why
we've crept back along these three
cruel centuries when so much grandeur beckons.
(It's the one scene not yet in our collection.)

Postmark: New York, April 19, 1912

Dear Father,
First, I want to thank you for keeping me
on the straight and narrow of £400 a year
in drizzly London, even though this means
my footman, butler, cook, and coachman
all answer to the same name. Which reminds
me, Harry says another £20 or so would
ensure he's not embarrassed by my scuffed
and wilted presence at the Royal Society.
Where, incidentally, I've already read three
papers, none of them to do with your dreaded
tariffs, but with what I dare hope could be
accepted soon as a new species of mole. I may
decline to name him eponymously despite
long tradition, but instead after William
Howard Taft, his blindness being remarkably
complete. But that's not why I write.
I'm sure you've heard by now of the fate
of RMS Titanic. I'd been in New York
for a lecture at the Museum of Natural History
on Kritosaurus, then set off on RMS Carpathia
for Fiume, where I'd got wind of a rare
Dalmatian Oligoporella, which to you might
be a mere fern but to me has all the inherent
grace of one of your balance sheets. Middle of
the third night, I felt us lurch round, then heat
stopped as we worked up speed. Everyone went
on deck, breaths swirling against the lamps,
the ship dodging floes until the boats went down
then returned loaded with women and children.
I served coffee and handed out blankets
for over four hours, then gave up my cabin
to a stunned woman frantic about her husband.
I've never before felt so grateful for your
patient support. You question if I'll ever make it
on my own steam. We black sheep are unsinkable.
With Sincere Appreciation,
Tom

**Postcard, Cornish Riviera Series:
Portsgatho, Nr. Falmouth, Cornwall, 1912**

Stonewall notch through curving
clifftop furze as a skirling
wind tunes heights to swirling
surf and the path to a few prim
cottages impossibly looms even
as it sings of least resistance.

Mother, I'd been dead for quite some
time but didn't realize until arriving here.
Suffocation is too strong a word for life
back home, but so is love. It's only cliffs
too beautiful to jump off that can cure you.
Or invite you to accept yourself just as you
are, incurable. Love as I've come to know
it is not giddy or confused or as described
in any Bible. Yet it's vertigo spun by this
very place that makes me risk this hand
across to you, asks you to leap. James

Postmark: Paris, August 2, 1914

Dear Father,
I'm sure you're eager to discover how things
stand here on the continent. No one who loves
these avenues as much as I, who's known their
subtle moods and charms could ever hope for war.
But duty to our firm compels me to assess things
with a clear eye. So much of Parisian life occurs by
sheer momentum that one has to learn to separate
waves from their deeper currents. The vendors at
Les Halles appear sanguine and continue buying in,
yet all the talk while giving change is of the previous
evening's papers, how the diplomats may put the brakes
on, but the onus lies with the Germans. Restaurants
are filled at night with patriotic songs, while streets
outside brim with conscripts headed for Gare de l'Est
and Gare du Nord. The young men in Cafés de Flore
and Deux Magots are adamant they'll make their point
by way of the bayonet then be back in time to watch
the camions roll in with the harvest. But I've witnessed
how they run things in Hamburg and Berlin—just
how we do them at our punctual little rolling mill.
I recommend considering expansion if the shells
start flying here. They'll need more before it's over.
Sincerely,
Charlie

Postmark: Compiègne, June 23, 1918

Dear Cousin Maddie,
I've meant to write sooner, since you've
no brothers and are therefore at the mercy
of the papers for news. Believe me when I say,
having seen it with my own two baby blues,
that what the Tribune prints is mainly lies. I hadn't
known until a fellow joined us in the front lines
as replacement, and it turned out we'd once been within
spitting distance of each other in New Haven. Except
that spit would have had to catch a good bit of Atlantic
Ocean breeze, since he's Italian and lived in West
Haven, while I was up at Yale. Anyway, he showed us
a copy of the paper bought on the docks in New York
right before his troop ship sailed, describing how we'd
"liberated" Cantigny from the Huns. Maddie, I was
there, crouching beside those Schneider tanks that look
like giant metal rhinos built on caterpillar tracks as our
guns kept the ground heaving just ahead of us. It took
half an hour to claim our prize: a pile of bricks
and timbers that had been a town. It was like a photo
I once saw taken after the great Chicago fire with just
a few hints as to how things had stood. Only I saw
a good deal more I won't go into. I just know whoever
kicked this lamp over has lots of explaining to do.
Yours Always,
Charlie

Postmark: Paris, September 6, 1918

Dear Father,
They finally gave us our week of leave
so we kicked up our soggy heels to beat
the band in Gay Paree. First night on the town
we wind up in a place without a single
mademoiselle, just us junior officer Maxim
gun fodder lined up at the bar like someone
dug a trench there, then filled it with cheap booze.
It's so bad we drink fast to forget the last
sip until the guy next to me, said he was from
some Carolina, starts slurring even worse
than the tar-paper drawl he started out with,
something about scent hounds and trees next
thing all hell breaks loose and a black
captain I hadn't noticed lunges across
two giant Boston Irish lugs to get at this guy.
Short story long, I got in some good swings
of my own, until the gendarmes swung in
and broke up the sharpest little action since
Verdun. Turns out that Carolina lout has
never sniffed the front. Turns out that captain's
in the old 15th New York and trained in
Spartanburg. Turns out they'd been in the lines
with les Poilus and given better than they got.
While I came here to bail out the French and got
bailed out by a guy our army says I can't salute.
Yours,
Tom

Postmark: New York, September 12, 1919

Dearest Aunt G,
I expect things are much the same out there
in sleepy Albuquerque. I have to tell you
about the parade we've just witnessed
all down 5th Avenue, flags big as thunderheads,
our troops—we call them "doughboys" now—
marching straight as arrows all the way back
to the docks at Le Havre. The Germans—we
call them "Bosch" here in New York—were
made short work of by Pershing, just like those
bandits who caused such trouble at our border
with Mexico. To see Old Glory waving block
after block made me almost sad the papers
say this was the war to end all wars. I may have
missed my chance to be kissed by an officer
who's not a titled gentleman, but means it.
Yours Always,
Sue

Historical Notes

SS City of New York was one of the great ocean liners of a 19th century in which transatlantic ships conveyed first-class passengers in splendor while generating profit for their owners by delivering third-class families from poorer parts of Europe to the mines, mills, and factories of the United States.

White Star flash refers to the famous White Star Line of British ships that rivaled the equally famous (and still operating) Cunard Line. RMS Titanic was a White Star vessel.

Lady Meux was the subject of several full-length portraits by James Abbott McNeil Whistler, an American painter originally from Lowell, Mass., who spent much of his life in Europe, and who is best known for his "Arrangement in Grey and Black No. 1," aka "Whistler's Mother."

Les Halles was for decades the main fresh food market of Paris. The iconic iron and glass building that was home to the market for more than a century was designed by the architect Victor Baltard in the 1850's.

Aristolochia is a hardy vine amenable to many climates and therefore an apt metaphor for social climbing in any era. During the Gilded Age, hundreds of American heiresses were shuttled to England by their socially aspirant parents to be married into to an English aristocracy in dire need of money to maintain its ancestral estates.

Longchamp is the scene of a racetrack in the Bois de Boulogne area of Paris that operates to the present day.

Giverny was chosen as the location of a typical French ancestral estate, one that might well have faced the choice between selling its artistic treasures and finding an American heiress who would forestall that unthinkable family humiliation.

Lillie Langtry was a socialite and actress celebrated mainly for her looks and personality, as well as her connections to a rapt male nobility.

As such, she was an early social media star.

Pont-Aven in the Brittany region of France was an artists' colony from the 1850's through the early 20th century. Many of its aspiring artists adopted their bold colors from Paul Gauguin, who painted there.

Barclays is one of London's most venerable banking institutions, established in 1690.

Gustave Sennelier opened his art supply store on the Left Bank of Paris in 1887. The Sennelier brand continues to the present day.

Trocadéro is an area of Paris across the Seine from the Eiffel Tower originally named after a French victory against Spain in 1823. The elaborate Palais du Trocadéro was intended as a place where international organizations could convene during the 1900 World's Fair.

"We'll soon try again for an heir"—producing a male heir was considered the primary "duty" of an American heiress married into English nobility.

Coronet is a simple crown, and a symbol of acceptance into minor English nobility.

Kid Gloves were de rigueur at dances and other social occasions that might result in a match of family aspirations and fortunes, preventing inappropriate skin-to-skin contact. They were made extremely thin and could be worn only once.

The Palais du Justice was built between 1857 and 1868 on the Îsle de La Cité, more famous as the site of the Notre Dame Cathedral, as part of the grand reconstruction of Paris carried out by the Emperor Napoleon III.

Paddington—one of the main train stations in London, operated by the Great Western Railway.

Duveen's refers to the famous art gallery of Joseph Duveen, who sold many European works of art to American businessmen with names such as Frick, Morgan, and Mellon.

Oxfordshire estate—an American woman married into the English nobility, especially one with her own aspirations and ideas, might well have found the routine of life at the country estate monotonous in comparison to the endless round of social and cultural events that characterized the London "season," where she had originally been introduced into English "society."

RMS Mauretania was another of the great transatlantic liners, and the world's largest ship when she was launched in 1906. She held the record for both fastest Eastbound and Westbound crossings, aka the "Blue Riband," for 20 years.

The great Philidor refers to François-André Danican Philidor (1726-1795), a chess master and comic opera composer still renowned for his "Philidor Defense."

Truculent cousins—Kaiser Wilhelm II of Germany, King George V of England, and Tsar Nicholas II of Russia were all cousins, which did not prevent them from sending millions of their countrymen to their deaths in battle against one another in WWI.

Saumur is the location of the military school that once trained French cavalry and still trains soldiers in reconnaissance and armored warfare. Cavalry tactics were swiftly made obsolete by the machine guns and trench systems of WWI.

Willie's Aintree Racing Colors recalls the 1885 election for the House of Commons (MP = Member of Parliament) in which Lord Randolph Churchill, having been appointed Secretary of State for India, was too busy with his new responsibilities to campaign. So his wife, Jennie Jerome (daughter of the Brooklyn financier Leonard Jerome and mother of Winston Churchill), did so on his behalf, traveling throughout his constituency to drum up votes and successfully staving off defeat. Aintree continues as the site of the famous "Grand National" steeplechase horserace to the present day.

Dear old Langham is the Langham Hotel, built between 1863 and 1865, and at the time the largest and most modern hotel in London. The incident involving Winston Churchill, known as the "Siege of Sidney Street," occurred in London's East End in 1911. It created controversy surrounding the direct intervention of Churchill, then the Home Secretary, after the military was called in by police to deal with two Latvian revolutionaries. And there was indeed an apparent scandal that had compelled the Jerome family to leave Brooklyn many years prior.

Ruelle Sourdis et Rue de Beauce seems a dreary scene for a postcard. However, postcards were a major contributor to the French economy, a phenomenon not so different from Instagram or Facebook today. By 1907, France was producing 300 million postcards a year. They were pasted into albums by collectors so avid that no scene was too unappealing or obscure to be sought after if it was also rare.

The Royal Society, founded in London in 1660, is the oldest scientific institution in the world.

Kritosaurus is a duck-billed dinosaur of the Late Cretaceous Period. Most of its fossil record remains missing,

RMS Carpathia was a Cunard Line passenger ship that came to the rescue of RMS Titanic, diverting all her steam power to her engines so as to arrive in time to retrieve 705 people from Titanic's lifeboats. She was torpedoed in July, 1918, by a German submarine.

Gare de l'Est and Gare du Nord are Paris train stations serving different regions of France, while **Café des Flore** and **Café du Magots** continue to serve Kir Royales to the present day.

Camion is the French word for "truck." Americans in France enjoyed using French parlance.

Cantigny was the first major American battle of WWI. Soldiers of the 28th Infantry Regiment leapt from their trenches after an hour-long artillery bombardment to follow a rolling barrage of exploding shells calculated to stay just ahead of the advancing troops. The French contributed Schneider tanks, early examples of their kind, designed to break the trench warfare deadlock. From a military standpoint, the battle was a complete success.

Maxim guns were the main German type of machine guns that, along with similar weapons developed by the French and British armies, were largely responsible for the carnage of trench warfare, as opposing armies tried unsuccessfully for years to cross "no man's land" and achieve a breakthrough. At the battle of the Somme, fought between July 1 and November 18, 1916, the British Army suffered over 415,000 casualties in a failed attempt to end the stalemate.

Les Poilus was a nickname given to the French infantry during WWI.

Verdun refers to the longest battle of WWI, fought between French and German forces, during which the combined armies endured 700,000 casualties over a period of ten months.

15th New York refers to the 15th National Guard Regiment, aka the 359th Infantry Regiment, aka the "Harlem Hellfighters." Because many white American soldiers refused to serve alongside African-Americans, the unit was issued French-made weapons and sent into the trenches with the French 16th Division. The unit earned a regimental Croix de Guerre, and also introduced jazz music to Europe via its regimental band.

Pershing is General John J. Pershing, aka "Black Jack Pershing," who led an expedition into Mexico in 1916 to capture the Mexican revolutionary general Pancho Villa that ultimately failed. Pershing proved more successful in France than he had been on the US-Mexico border.

Ed Granger's first chapbook, *Glasshouse*, was a finalist in the Cape Cod Poetry Review Chapbook Contest. Growing up in a house with an extensive library of classic literature fed his lifelong love affair with language. He was also raised to appreciate music and the visual arts, and earned a degree from Berklee College of Music in Boston. Subsequently, he worked as a sportswriter in the Boston area, winning several awards. For over two decades, he has lived in the Pennsylvania farm country where he grew up, and where he is now helping to raise a teenage daughter. In addition to the arts, his interests include history, a wide range of spiritual traditions, and the American philosophical tradition from Emerson through William James, John Dewey, and Jane Addams, to Cornel West.

www.ingramcontent.com/pod-product-compliance
Lightning Source LLC
LaVergne TN
LVHW041505070426
835507LV00012B/1329